GREAT FILMMAKERS
KATHRYN BIGELOW

Susan Dudley Gold

Cavendish
Square

New York

Published in 2015 by Cavendish Square Publishing, LLC
243 5th Avenue, Suite 136, New York, NY 10016

Copyright © 2015 by Cavendish Square Publishing, LLC

First Edition

CPSIA Compliance Information: Batch #WS14CSQ

All websites were available and accurate when this book was sent to press.

Library of Congress Cataloging-in-Publication Data
Gold, Susan Dudley.
Kathryn Bigelow / Susan Dudley Gold.
   pages cm. — (Great filmmakers)
Includes index.
ISBN 978-1-62712-939-8 (hardcover) ISBN 978-1-62712-941-1 (ebook)
1. Bigelow, Kathryn—Juvenile literature. 2. Motion picture producers and directors—United States—Biography—Juvenile literature. I. Title.
PN1998.3.B565G65 2014
791.43'0233'092—dc23
[B]
                          2014001530

Editorial Director: Dean Miller   Designer: Amy Greenan
Editor: Fletcher Doyle   Production Manager: Jennifer Ryder-Talbot
Copy Editor: Cynthia Roby   Production Editor: David McNamara
Art Director: Jeffrey Talbot   Photo Researcher: J8 Media

The photographs in this book are used by permission and through the courtesy of: Cover, 1, Jason LaVeris/FilmMagic/Getty Images; Jason Merritt/Getty Images, 5; Martha Holmes/Time & Life Pictures/Getty Images, 7; Ebet Roberts/Redferns/Getty Images, 9; Herve GLOAGUEN/ Gamma-Rapho/Getty Images, 13; pagadesign/E+/Getty Images, 14, 22, 44, 64; www.demilked. com/free-paper-textures-backgrounds, 14–15, 22, 44–45, 64–65; David Corio/Redferns/Getty Images, 15; Bob Riha Jr/WireImage/Getty Images, 17; Michael Ochs Archives/Moviepix/ Getty Images, 19; Bennett Raglin/WireImage/Getty Images, 22; Hulton Archive/Moviepix/ Getty Images, 25; Michael Buckner/WireImage/Getty Images, 26; © Moviestore Collection Ltd/ Alamy, 29; Fotos International/Archive Photos/Getty Images, 30; © AF archive/Alamy, 31; Time & Life Pictures/Getty Images, 33; 20TH CENTURY FOX/ Album/Newscom, 34; Archive Photos/ Moviepix/Getty Images, 35; AP Photo/Eric Draper, 37; © AF archive/Alamy, 39; © Moviestore Collection Ltd/Alamy, 40; Frank Micelotta/Getty Images, 43; GABRIEL BOUYS/ AFP/Getty Images, 45; Jürg Carstensen/picture-alliance/dpa/AP Images, 47; © AF archive/ Alamy, 49; Matt Carr/Getty Images, 50; AP Photo/Dan Steinberg, 52; © AF archive/Alamy, 54; Jordan Strauss/Invision/AP Images, 57; Michael Caulfield/WireImage/Getty Images, 58; STRDEL/AFP/Getty Images, 61; Columbia Pictures/Unimedia Images, Inc./Columbia Pictures/ Newscom, 65; Christopher Polk/BAFTA LA/Getty Images, 67.

Printed in the United States of America

GREAT FILMMAKERS
KATHRYN BIGELOW

1 EARLY YEARS

The star-studded audience gathered at the Kodak Theatre in Hollywood fell silent. Barbra Streisand quickly opened the envelope that held the name of the winner of the 2010 Academy Award for best **director**. After a brief pause to read the name silently, Streisand exclaimed: "Well, the time has come." Then she announced the winner to the world: Kathryn Bigelow, the first—and, as of 2014, the only—woman ever to win the prestigious award. The audience broke into wild applause. Streisand, who has also directed several films, raised her arms in triumph.

Accepting the Oscar for directing her film *The Hurt Locker*, Bigelow appeared stunned. "It's the moment of a lifetime," she told the audience. "This is so extraordinary to be in the company of ... such powerful filmmakers, who have inspired me and [whom] I have admired for decades."

Helen Reddy's *I am Woman* accompanied Bigelow's exit from the stage. The song, the

Oscar winner Bigelow with presenter Barbra Streisand in 2010.

unofficial anthem for the women's liberation movement, highlighted the toppling of another barrier for females. Lina Wertmuller in 1976, Jane Campion in 1993, and Sofia Coppola in 2003 are the only other women directors to be nominated for an Oscar. Bigelow said she "longed for the day" when women would be known only as directors, not as female directors.

Her movies—intense and action-packed—depict just how seductive violence can be. Bigelow's films also exhibit the artistic touch of a director who is a talented painter. Panoramic landscapes and glowing, sun-soaked skies fill the screens. Art and gore, complicated heroes, shades of good and evil, and intense action—are all marks of a Bigelow film.

Kathryn Ann Bigelow was born November 27, 1951 in San Carlos, California, a town located midway between San Francisco and San Jose. An only child, she began painting when she was six. Part of her desire to become an artist came from her father, a manager at a local paint factory, who drew cartoons for her. Bigelow later told *Newsweek* that her father never achieved his dream of being a professional cartoonist, and that inspired her to push harder toward her goal of becoming an artist. Her mother was a librarian. Bigelow described her home life as "a fairly normal environment."

During her childhood, Bigelow considered herself an outsider, mainly because of her height: she is almost six feet tall. She said that her classmates seemed "more normal" than she was. To escape, she sought out the company of horses, which she still loves to ride. She also created her own world in her drawings.

Bigelow did not set out to be a film director. After graduating from high school, she studied painting

The work of abstract expressionist painter Jackson Pollock was a big influence on Kathryn as she developed artistically.

for two years at the San Francisco Art Institute, a school that focuses on **contemporary art** and has long encouraged students to experiment in various mediums. In the years Bigelow attended the institute (1969–1971), students had begun exploring **performance art** and **conceptual art**. Performance art combines visual art and dramatic presentation. Conceptual art zeroes in on the ideas behind the art rather than on the artwork itself. Students used photography, film, music, and other media as well as more traditional artwork and sculpture in their presentations.

Painting on giant canvases, Bigelow worked in oil and specialized in **abstract expressionism**—an art **form** that uses abstract images (those that do not resemble real objects or people) to evoke emotional feelings. In some of her work from this time, Bigelow used a small detail from a painting by fifteenth-century Italian painter Raphael—a foot or a hand—and magnified it until it filled her canvas. She then painted it as an abstract image. Jackson Pollock and Willem de Kooning among others became famous for their use of the art form. They, and other artists, made New York City the international center of abstract expressionism beginning in the 1940s and 1950s.

After two years at the San Francisco Art Institute, Bigelow set her sights on New York City, which had remained the international center of abstract expressionism. Without her knowledge, one of her professors sent slides of her work to the Whitney Museum of American Art—a New York institution known for its support of living American artists. As a result, twenty-year-old Bigelow was awarded a painting scholarship to the museum's Independent Study Program.

Composer Philip Glass renovated New York City lofts with Bigelow while both were struggling artists in the 1970s.

"Never Happier"

In New York Bigelow joined the ranks of struggling artists. Her new home was a makeshift studio inside an abandoned bank vault under a branch of a former Off Track Betting building. She slept in a sleeping bag to keep warm. At night, gunshots could often be heard in the gritty streets of the neighborhood. Yet Bigelow said she was "never happier." Susan Sontag, the author and essayist, became Bigelow's creative advisor. Designer and landscape architect Vito Acconci and sculptor Richard Serra viewed her work at the Whitney studios. Philip Glass, who had not yet gained fame as one of America's most influential composers, joined her circle of friends. To earn money, Bigelow and Glass, who also drove taxis, converted old buildings into artist lofts. The lofts, located in the city's SoHo and Tribeca neighborhoods, had once been print factories. Glass installed the plumbing; Bigelow covered the walls in sheetrock and sanded the floors, which had been stained with years of spilled ink. They lived in the buildings as they worked. Once the renovations were complete, they turned the space over to new tenants, who paid them. Photographer Robert Mapplethorpe rented an apartment in the building where Bigelow lived.

Bigelow shared her thoughts on art and philosophy with a community of artists who lived and worked nearby. The artists in her circle worked with many different forms. Bigelow and her friends experimented with painting, acting, dance, video, music, and philosophical writing. Vito Acconci hired her to make films, which he used as background for his gallery shows.

Bigelow was drawn to conceptual art. One of her early works made use of large metal pipes she found on the streets of New York. She gathered the pipes and rolled them across the metal flooring of her bank vault/studio. They clanged together and produced tones that echoed throughout the space. Bigelow recorded the sounds and played the tape as people viewed her collection of pipes. "I guess it was about a sense of what's possible," she told *Time* magazine years later.

While in New York, Bigelow connected with a group known as Art & Language, which challenged the "limitations" of traditional art. Members believed that traditional art was fully accessible only to elitists. They argued that art should be open to everyday people. Lawrence Weiner, a key figure in the conceptual art world, became Bigelow's mentor at the Whitney. Pop artist Andy Warhol, also a friend of Bigelow's, reinforced the idea that traditional art excluded many people. He noted that movies were much easier to view. A moviegoer did not have to travel to a specific museum and have knowledge of a certain art form in order to see and enjoy a movie.

The idea appealed to Bigelow. Some of her conceptual artist friends worked in film, and Bigelow began to make short films, or **shorts**, with them. She also appeared in several short conceptual art films and videos that she helped make Weiner in the 1970s. These artists influenced her work. Bigelow later told *Artforum*: "I became dissatisfied with the art world—the fact that it requires a certain amount of knowledge to appreciate abstract material."

Film as a Canvas

Film became Bigelow's new canvas. In the late 1970s she was awarded a grant from the **National Endowment for the Arts** to produce a short movie. She filmed the short in an alley not far from where she lived at the time. The characters—two conceptual artist friends—spend the entire film beating each other. At the end, the two men kiss. Bigelow's lack of experience in filmmaking showed in the bruises her friends endured. She did not know how to direct them to deliver fake punches, so her friends supplied the real thing.

Bigelow ran out of money before she could edit the film. With hopes of getting funding, she sent the uncut footage to the film school at Columbia University. Milos Forman, a famous director who taught at the school, liked Bigelow's work so much that he offered her a scholarship. She eventually produced the film, which she titled *The Set-Up*, to meet her senior course requirements. The Whitney presented the film in 1978.

The twenty-minute film contains no dialogue. Instead Bigelow plays a recording of two professors discussing the philosophical meaning of the fighters' punches. The film is a study in violence and why it is so seductive to viewers. The allure of violence would figure prominently in her future films.

Bigelow earned a master's degree in fine arts from New York City's Columbia University in 1979. Although she later taught film classes at the university, her main interest was making movies. While still at Columbia she connected with fellow student Monty Montgomery. Together they wrote a script about bikers who invade a small Southern town while on their way to Daytona Beach. The film was inspired by a 1954 outlaw biker movie starring Marlon Brando: *The Wild One*. Bigelow and Montgomery titled the work *U.S. 17*, the road the bikers followed. The pair codirected the movie.

During her search for a lead actor, Bigelow saw Willem Dafoe perform on stage in New York. Dafoe, then twenty-five, immediately accepted Bigelow's offer to star in her film. It was Dafoe's first major film role, as well as Bigelow's first feature film.

In September 1980, Bigelow and Montgomery began shooting the movie in Georgia off Route 17. As the movie opens, Dafoe as Vance, the bad-boy biker, rides along the highway. He stops to change a flat tire for a woman who is drawn to his rebel looks. He changes her tire, but maintains his bad boy image when he steals her money and forces her to kiss him. Vance stops at a roadside luncheonette to wait for his biker friends. He flirts with the

Artist Andy Warhol suggested that Bigelow think about film as an "accessible" art form.

waitress but the other patrons feel threatened by his presence. When his buddies arrive, the sense of danger intensifies. Filming took twenty-five days.

Bigelow uses the screen as her palette. The soft pastels of the peach luncheonette's booths, the pink dress worn by the waitress, and the chartreuse dress of the woman motorist contrast sharply with the black leather worn by the bikers. The threat of violence casts a dark shadow over the town. This early movie had little dialogue and focused more on the characters and mood than on plot.

Bigelow and Montgomery renamed their film *Breakdown* before its world premiere, at the

IN FRONT OF THE CAMERA

TITLE

DIRECTOR

CAMERA

DATE **SCENE** **TAKE**

Kathryn Bigelow usually works behind the camera, directing the action. But on rare occasions she has appeared in front of the lens. She is famous for being the only major director to have appeared in a Gap ad. Early in her career, she acted in a 1974 Richard Serra film titled *Prisoners Dilemma,* in which she played the role of a district attorney's assistant.

Bigelow appeared in *Born in Flames,* a science fiction film produced and directed by Lizzie Borden in 1983. Her role in the documentary-style film was that of a feminist newspaper editor. She played the role of another strong woman in a 1988 cowboy-biker music video for **New Wave** band Martini Ranch. The band featured actor Bill Paxton, who sang, and Andrew Todd Rosenthal, who played the guitar and supplied vocals. In it, Bigelow portrays the tough leader of a group of cowgirl bounty hunters chasing a gang of bank robbers led

Bigelow's mentor, artist and filmmaker Richard Serra, among his sculptures in the MOMA Sculpture Garden in New York.

by Paxton. Actors Judge Reinhold and Paul Reiser also appear in the video. James Cameron, Bigelow's then-future husband (married 1989-1991), directed the seven-minute video, *Reach*.

Bigelow helped produce a music video with the Red Krayola, an experimental band of the 1960s and 1970s. She also directed a video in 1987 for the English rock band New Order titled *Touched by the Hand of God*, which mocked the ultra-glamorous music videos of the day.

Festival del Film Locarno in Switzerland on August 18, 1981. The movie had its premiere in the United States at the Los Angeles International Film Exposition on March 27, 1982. For the event the filmmakers renamed the film again, this time, *The Loveless*. It opened in New York at the Waverly Theater in January 1984. The gala marking the New York premiere attracted people prominent in the city's art scene, including Bigelow's friends, Robert Mapplethorpe and Andy Warhol. Critics gave the movie mixed reviews.

Janet Maslin, a movie critic for the *New York Times*, slammed *The Loveless*, describing it as "a pathetic homage to the 1950s." The critic found the film to be "painfully slow" and said the bikers were hotshots, not "menacing invaders."

Other reviewers found enjoyable elements in Bigelow's first film. A critic writing for London's *Time Out* called it "one of the most original American independents in years: a bike movie which celebrates the '50s through '80s eyes." Although admitting that the slow pace could be irritating, the critic praised the film's "super-saturated atmosphere." For the most part, filmgoers gave the movie a pass. However, it caught the attention of Walter Hill, who convinced Universal Studios to offer Bigelow a deal to develop a film. Bigelow accepted and moved to Hollywood in 1983. When nothing came of the deal, Bigelow began teaching at the California Institute of the Arts.

A young Willem Dafoe played Vance in Bigelow's first feature film, *The Loveless*.

2 VAMPIRES AND COPS

Five years after the U.S. premiere of *The Loveless*, Kathryn Bigelow delivered her first solo-directing effort. In her 1987 film *Near Dark*, Bigelow combined horror and western genres. The movie centers on a young rancher who is seduced by a beautiful girl vampire and then kidnapped by her redneck vampire clan. Cowboy hats and a white horse compete with gore and violence in this film. Bigelow wrote the script with Eric Red in 1986. Red, a twenty-six-year-old screenwriter based out of Los Angeles, had written the script for a highway horror film, *The Hitcher*, the year before.

Bigelow and Red produced *Near Dark* without the backing of a major film studio. That increased the financial risk, but Bigelow told *New York Times* reporter Jamie Diamond that the arrangement gave her more control over the film and its outcome.

At the time Bigelow had little money. "I had like half a can of tuna fish and a bottle of stale water in the refrigerator and that was it," she later said during

Some of the *Near Dark* cast.

a conversation with other directors organized by the *Los Angeles Times*. A **producer** offered to buy the script, but Bigelow had written it so that she would have a film to direct—so she turned him down. Bigelow then convinced independent producer Steven-Charles Jaffe to finance the $5 million film with her as director.

Much of the cast, including Bill Paxton and Jenette Goldstein as vampires Severen and Diamondback, had acted in James Cameron's movie *Aliens*, released in 1986. In the opening scenes, cowboy Caleb Colton, played by Adrian Pasdar, meets Mae, a beautiful young girl played by Jenny Wright. He is captivated by her. When she asks for a ride, he agrees to take her in his truck. But when he kisses her, she bites his neck. He tries to get away, but his truck won't start. As he runs through the fields toward his home, it becomes apparent that Mae's bite has turned him into a vampire. The rising sun burns his skin. Mae's clan of vampires drives up in a van and pulls him inside. The van's blackened windows provide protection from the killer sun.

Weird Vampires and Black Humor

The vampire family Caleb joins is a weird bunch. In addition to Mae, the clan includes an old vampire played by Lance Henriksen, as well as the angry big-haired Diamondback, Homer—a "boy" who is actually more than a century old (Joshua John Miller)—and the hot-tempered, wild-eyed Severen.

The action follows the vampire clan through violent nights of killing and feasting on blood. When Caleb refuses to kill, Mae shares her ration of the blood all vampires depend on to live. They fall in love, and the rest of the vampires grudgingly give him a week to prove himself a member of the clan. Meanwhile, Caleb's father is desperately trying to find his kidnapped son. The movie is filled with black humor. When Caleb first meets Mae, he innocently asks her for a bite of her ice cream cone. She teasingly repeats, "Bite?" Later, Severen bites into a victim at a bar and then complains, "I hate it when they ain't been shaved."

Bigelow humanized her characters by employing humor throughout the script. This helped audiences relate to the vampires in *Near Dark* even as they sucked the blood from their victims. "Humor is very important when you're dealing with violence," Bigelow told a reporter for the **genre** magazine *Cinemafantastique*, which publishes reviews on horror, fantasy, and science fiction films. "I like the sense of watching something horrific and having fun with it and not quite understanding why you're having fun with it. I think that's interesting."

As in her other movies, Bigelow uses color and light to set the mood in *Near Dark*. To capture the harsh lighting of the desert, the filming took place in Arizona as well as California and Oklahoma. Dark velvet night skies contrast with harsh orange suns. During a shoot-out at a motel, the sun streams in through each bullet hole in the walls. Those seeping rays of light—deadly to the vampires— intensify the sense of danger.

Bigelow uses slow motion to build the pressure as Caleb, set on fire by the sun, runs to the van. His rescue of Mae and the rest of the vampires helps secure his place in the clan. When Caleb's vampire family meets his real kin, he faces a terrible choice. His dilemma is resolved with an ingenious twist, and the film has a happy ending.

BIGELOW THE ARTIST

Violence and vampires aside, the movie *Near Dark* brought attention to Bigelow the artist. The silhouetted scenes of characters against the Western sky at sunrise and sunset are as beautiful as museum landscapes. Film critic Owen Gleiberman praised Bigelow's "shimmering vampire Western," which he described as "a gorgeous example of style for style's sake." Jay Boyar, movie critic for the *Orlando Sentinel*, made note of Bigelow's art training and her "dusky, shadowy style."

The Museum of Modern Art (MOMA) in New York paid homage to Bigelow's filmmaking talent in 1988 by adding her work to its collection. MOMA curator Larry Kardish said the museum considered Bigelow to be "a significant talent," adding that her use of color, light, and dark to establish the atmosphere in her films set her apart from other filmmakers.

But the lure of violence is there—a theme Bigelow uses repeatedly.

The movie runs ninety-five minutes. In it, Bigelow wastes no time on the usual trappings of the vampire world: fangs, garlic, or crosses. The characters are not even referred to as vampires. *Near Dark* succeeds, though, in creeping out the viewer while telling a love story at the same time. Director Oliver Stone, marveling at the film's intensity, once called the movie "a horror **haiku**."

A Cult Favorite

Again, Bigelow earned mixed reviews. *New York Times* critic Caryn James found fault with *Near Dark*'s "unconvincing special effects." She wrote: "Some vampires walk around with a little blood around their mouths, but it's as if they're messy eaters—disgusting but not exactly horrifying."

On the other hand, *Variety* credited Bigelow with achieving "a new look in vampire films." The entertainment news magazine also noted that the movie was "the most hard-edged, violent [action movie] ever directed by an American woman."

Bigelow faced severe setbacks in distributing *Near Dark*. The first distribution deal fell through. The company that took over went bankrupt in the middle of releasing the film. At its peak, the movie ran in only 429 theaters. It eventually brought in $3.4 million, well below its $5 million production cost. Even so, *Near Dark* appealed to fans of science fiction and horror. Its seductive violence and visual effects boosted it to cult status soon after it was released as a video in 1988. Despite Bigelow's growing reputation for originality and rich visuals, she had yet to produce a film that was a commercial success.

A Film with Real Blood

Near Dark caught the attention of two leaders in the film industry: director Oliver Stone and producer Edward Pressman. Stone sought out Bigelow even before the release of *Near Dark* because he had heard she was "an unusual talent." After viewing Bigelow's vampire movie, Stone said that he was so impressed by its intensity that he asked to participate in her next effort. "I was surprised by the inherent ferocity of her work," he said. "She has a relentlessness that I think is masculine."

Pressman, an independent producer, was also a Bigelow fan. Bigelow "was trying to push the [film] form as far as she could," he told a reporter for the *Los Angeles Times*. At Stone's urging, Pressman agreed to coproduce Bigelow's next film, *Blue Steel*, with him.

Bigelow and Eric Red joined forces again to write the script. Bigelow cast Jamie Lee Curtis as the lead character, Megan Turner, a rookie police detective on the trail of a psychotic killer. Louise Fletcher, an **Oscar**-winning actress, played the role of Turner's mother. It was the first time Bigelow had used major stars in a production. *Blue Steel* also marked Bigelow's acceptance by the major studios when MGM agreed to distribute the film.

Although Bigelow enjoyed the freedom of working with independent producers, she wanted to expand beyond the small, dedicated audiences who viewed her previous films. That meant producing films that major studios would support. She told *Los Angeles*

Jamie Lee Curtis in *Blue Steel*.

Times reporter Clarke Taylor that she knew she needed to attract more moviegoers to keep working as a director. "I can't just ask for money to fulfill my own creative desires. And yet I want to be able to continue to make films I can live with," she said.

Blue Steel aimed at a broader audience—Bigelow and Red created a reality-based thriller. "When people bleed in this film," Jamie Lee Curtis told Taylor, "they really bleed." Bigelow introduced a new twist to the action thriller by putting a tough but flawed woman cop at its center. Certainly it was a first: a woman directing an action film with a woman as the main character. Yet *Blue Steel* did not fall short of the level of intensity and violence present in Bigelow's previous films.

In the movie's early scenes, a clearly scared Turner witnesses an armed robbery at a grocery store. It is her first day on the job and she shoots the robber dead. One of the shoppers, Eugene Hunt, a wealthy **commodities trader** played by Ron Silver, secretly grabs the robber's gun and disappears. Turner is suspended when it appears she shot an unarmed man.

Soon she joins her fellow officers in the hunt for a psychotic killer who is shooting people all over town. Each bullet has Turner's name carved into it. She has no idea that the suave guy she is dating, the commodities trader from the robbery scene, is the killer. When she discovers the truth, he begins targeting her friends and family. The heroine's inner strength is tested throughout the film. She is not a passive victim—she fights back. In the end, she is driven to break the law herself.

Director James Cameron and Kathryn Bigelow.

The filming of *Blue Steel* took about two months (August to October 1988). Bigelow shot the entire movie in New York City. Filming on location can be far more challenging than in a studio. Bigelow estimated that two million people walked by as her crew shot scenes along Wall Street. One scene was shot on the trading floor of the New York Mercantile Exchange in Manhattan. A trader, unaware that Bigelow was filming, attempted to trade with the actor portraying Hunt. He was shocked when she called, "Cut."

When Bigelow returned to Hollywood to work on the film, director James Cameron visited *Blue Steel* headquarters to scout for actors for his movies. During the visit, Cameron met Bigelow. He had recently split from his second wife, producer Gale Hurd. The two directors fell for each other and married shortly afterward (August 1989). Though the marriage lasted only two years, the two have continued to collaborate on films.

Intense and violent, *Blue Steel* is a psychological thriller framed by Bigelow's trademark artistic vision. "She paints with light, rather than just lighting a set," Curtis said of Bigelow's filming style. In the opening credits, Bigelow focuses on an extremely close shot of what looks like a rolling blue landscape. It turns out to be the blue steel of Curtis's gun.

Blue Steel premiered in the United States in March 1990. It attracted attention among reviewers for its handling of characters and its nonstop suspense. Film critic Roger Ebert praised the film's "intriguing characters." He noted that *Blue Steel* had all the marks of a traditional thriller. The movie, he said, had "one shock and surprise after another," with "a couple of superior examples of the killer-jumping-unexpectedly-from-the-dark scene."

Kenneth Turan, film critic for the *Los Angeles Times*, agreed. "Bigelow is emerging as one of the peerless action/suspense directors of her generation," he wrote. *Entertainment Weekly*'s critic Owen Gleiberman criticized the film's slow pace but praised its "fever-dream clarity" and hard-hitting action. Critic Nigel Floyd, writing for *Time Out*, London's cultural guide, called the movie "seductively stylish." The film, he said, proved "that a woman can enter a traditionally male world and, like Megan, beat men at their own game."

Audiences responded well to the film. With an estimated budget of $6 million to $7 million, the movie took in more than $8 million. It was shown in 1,307 theaters nationwide, thereby gaining Bigelow a much wider audience.

3 COLLABORATIONS WITH CAMERON

For her next movie, Bigelow teamed with her husband, James Cameron. They delivered *Point Break*, a surfer/skydiver action extravaganza. The two wrote the script, which was based on a screenplay written by W. Peter Iliff. Cameron produced the movie, while Bigelow served as its director. The film was released after the couple's divorce in 1991. Working with an estimated $24 million budget, Bigelow took special effects to great lengths. She created huge vistas of ocean and sky. The movie is named for the surfing term used to describe a wave that breaks as it strikes a point of land, then wraps around the point.

The movie opens with a scene shot from the viewpoint of a group of robbers as they drive toward the bank they have targeted. At first the audience has no idea what is happening. The robbers don masks of four former Presidents—Lyndon Johnson, Ronald Reagan, Richard Nixon, and Jimmy Carter.

Bigelow on location for the *Point Break* shoot in 1991.

Keanu Reeves and Patrick Swayze on the beach in *Point Break*, 1991.

They enter the bank, pull off the heist in ninety seconds, and make a fast getaway.

Keanu Reeves stars as Johnny Utah, a young FBI agent. Utah and his partner, Angelo Pappas (played by Gary Busey), suspect that the gang is headed by Bodhi, a master surfer played by Patrick Swayze. To track the robbers, Utah learns to surf. He is drawn to Bodhi and his quest for excitement. In one sequence, Utah chases the robber in the Reagan mask (Bodhi) on a dizzying race along streets and through houses. Bigelow developed a special camera, one lighter than standard equipment, to shoot the chase scene. She shifts the camera so that the audience views the action from the point of view of the runners. This technique, a favorite Bigelow trademark, serves to plunge the audience directly into the action.

Adrenaline Rush

The adrenaline rush that flows in many Bigelow movies comes on strong in *Point Break* as she presents one over-the-top sequence after another. At the beginning of the chase scene, Bodhi, as Ronald Reagan, uses a gas pump as a flamethrower. In another, Utah jumps from a plane without a parachute to grab Bodhi as he rockets to the ground. Utah pulls the chute's cord just in time. The result is an action-packed, extreme-sports movie with strong characters and gorgeous **cinematography**. To get the shots of the surf, Bigelow sat in a boat "as close as I could be without getting in the shot." For close-ups she sat on a surfboard and yelled action before falling into the waves. During the skydiving scenes, Bigelow was strapped into the plane wearing a parachute of her own. Unlike the movie's characters, however, she did not jump.

The four "presidents" as bank robbers.

Distributed by 20th Century Fox, *Point Break* was a big-time hit for Bigelow. It was first released in the United States on July 12, 1991. The movie took in $83.5 million worldwide and was shown in 1,625 U.S. theaters. Rentals brought in an additional $49 million worldwide.

Some critics were as enthusiastic as the audiences while others were not. Roger Ebert awarded the movie three and a half stars out of four. He called Bigelow a "gifted filmmaker." Ebert warned viewers not to take the story line too seriously. The plot, he said, was "preposterous," yet the film's action-packed scenes were "surprisingly effective." The characters, too, had an "intriguing" side to them. "They aren't men of action, but men of thought who choose action as a way of expressing their beliefs," Ebert wrote in a review of the film. A *Time Out* critic noted: "There's enough high-octane, heart-racing excitement for a dozen movies." Other critics, however, slammed the movie.

Variety called it "a hare-brained wild ride through big surf and bad vibes." Hal Hinson, critic for the *Washington Post* said the film was "gorgeous but dumb as a post." Overall, the movie received enough attention from fans to push it to cult status. A remake of the film by Alcon Entertainment is scheduled for release in 2015. With an estimated $100 million budget, the film will include other extreme sports in addition to surfing. Alcon chose Ericson Core to direct the new film.

Point Break strengthened Bigelow's reputation as one of the leading directors of action thrillers. For the moment, at least, she appeared on Hollywood's list of top directors. *New York Times* film critic Janet Maslin noted that Bigelow had a real talent "as a director of fast-paced, high-adrenaline action."

She also became known for dark films with flawed characters, and at times, disturbing violence. Such material attracted her, she told interviewer Victoria Hamburg in 1989. "It has an energy; it's very provocative," she said, adding, "I think it's important to challenge."

Ralph Fiennes, star of Bigelow's *Strange Days*, pictured with Liam Neeson.

Real Life Uncut

The characters and science fiction premise of her next film, *Strange Days*, challenged viewers and critics alike. The film, another joint project with Cameron, takes place just before the turn of the twenty-first century. Helmeted police patrol a riot-torn Los Angeles. In this vision of the future, high-tech gadgets called "Superconducting Quantum Interference Devices" (SQUIDs) record every detail of an event, right down to the emotions and reactions of the people involved. Viewers can actually experience the feelings of others. The lead, Lenny Nero, played by Ralph Fiennes, is a sleazy ex-cop who sells clips of the recordings to bored businessmen. Wearing viewing caps, they participate in random high-risk acts that include violence without the danger of the real thing. "This is real life,

Bigelow on set directing 1995's *Strange Days.*

pure and uncut, straight from the cerebral cortex," Lenny says.

Like the recorded clips, *Strange Days* draws the audience into a world of violence and suspense. One recording captures the murder of a black rap artist named Jeriko One by two Los Angeles cops. Iris, a friend of Lenny's, records the killing by mistake. She runs from the cops and tosses the clip into Lenny's car. Shortly afterward, someone records the rape and murder of Iris and sends the clip to Lenny. Moviegoers see the awful events from Iris's point of view as well as that of her killer. Bigelow's shifting camera angles bring the violence disturbingly close to the audience. The director uses lightweight handheld cameras to allow quick movements in small spaces. This shows the action from different angles, mirroring the way action is captured by the human eye.

Actors Angela Bassett and Ralph Fiennes.

Angela Bassett plays the tough limo driver Mace who loves Lenny and protects him as he runs from the cops. Meanwhile, Lenny tries to rescue his ex-girlfriend Faith, played by Juliette Lewis, from her new boyfriend, Philo. Lenny becomes addicted to the clips that recorded his love affair with Faith. Through most of the film, he tries to get her back. In the end, he weans himself off the virtual reality of the clips. He opens his eyes to real life and joins Mace to unmask the killers of Jeriko One and Iris.

Cameron had considered filming the story behind *Strange Days* off and on for nine years. Finally, in 1991, he showed it to Bigelow, who immediately saw its potential. Cameron and Jay Cocks, who was a film critic for *Time* magazine, produced the script. He had worked with Bigelow on an earlier script about Joan of Arc. The project fell through, however, when she and the producer disagreed over who would take on the starring role.

Like Bigelow's other films, *Strange Days* was produced without the backing of Hollywood's big studios. Cameron gave his considerable support to the project along with producer Steven-Charles Jaffe.

Strange Days received mixed reviews. *San Francisco Chronicle* critic Edward Guthmann called the film an "adrenaline feed." He wrote that it was as if Bigelow "had vowed to out-macho Oliver Stone: to lift us to fever pitch, hold us suspended and blast us with cinematic overkill."

Others believed the director took the violence in the film too far. Both critics and audiences denounced Bigelow's handling of the violent acts committed against Iris. At some showings of the film, audience members walked out during the scene. Many thought the film, by highlighting the violence, was as depraved as the clips sold in the movie. Some accused Bigelow of exploiting women. The audience also did not respond well to the role reversals of Mace, the woman hero, and Lenny, the man who needs rescuing.

Movie insiders, though, recognized the skill and talent that went into creating the film. For the first time the American Academy of Science Fiction, Fantasy & Horror Films awarded its Saturn Award for best director to a woman, Kathryn Bigelow, for her work on *Strange Days.* The film also earned nominations for best actor, best science fiction film, and best writing from the academy. Angela Bassett won the Saturn Award for best actress.

Even with such acclaim, the movie did not do well at the **box office**. With an estimated budget of $42 million, the film **grossed** less than $8 million. This loss caused Bigelow, who had been near the top of Hollywood's director list, to fall out of favor with the big studios.

During this time Bigelow kept busy with smaller projects. She directed episodes of the television series *Homicide: Life on the Streets*, a gritty show about cops in Baltimore. Bigelow also directed an

36

episode of *Wild Palms*, a sci-fi mini-series that dealt with the misuse of mass media. Oliver Stone was executive producer of the show.

Bigelow teamed with Eric Red yet again to write the script for a psychological thriller, *Undertow*, released in 1996. Red directed the film, which revolves around three characters threatened by a hurricane. Critics panned the TV movie.

The Santa Monica Freeway split apart near the La Cienega overpass after a major quake struck the Los Angeles basin.

On January 17, 1994, Bigelow experienced disaster in her own life. An earthquake struck Santa Monica—the freeway collapsed. Fifty-seven people died and 8,700 suffered injuries. The event caused an estimated $20 million in damages. The quake destroyed Bigelow's house, where she had lived with James Cameron during their marriage and which she retained after the divorce. It took her twenty months to rebuild the home, which was perched on a hillside. She shares the house with her two energetic German shepherds.

4 DIMINISHING RETURNS

After the release of *Strange Days*, five years passed before Bigelow directed her next film, *The Weight of Water*. It is based on a novel of the same name by Anita Shreve. Part historical fiction, part modern-day tale of a marriage going bad, the movie marked a big change for Bigelow. Instead of the violent action that dominated her previous films, *The Weight of Water* focuses on five women and their struggles. The film seesaws between two stories: one that takes place during the 1870s, and the other, present-day. The events in the past were based on an actual murder.

Critic Emanual Levy (*Variety*) called the film Bigelow's "most ambitious and personal work to date." Other favorable reviews said the film was "uncommonly intelligent and uncompromising" and praised the "vibrant and rock-solid" performances of its stars. But others criticized the slow pace and the sudden shifts in time. Gary Dowell in the *Dallas Morning News* faulted the movie's "jarring jumps

Bigelow on the set of *K-19: The Widowmaker*.

The Weight of Water stars Sarah Polley and Vinessa Shaw.

between disconnected stories" and its "watered-down sensationalism."

The Weight of Water cost about $16 million to produce, a modest amount in the world of multimillion-dollar films, but it did not click with fans of Bigelow's usual action-oriented films. The movie's return was a paltry $109,130. It screened in only twenty-seven theaters and ended its run after three weeks.

Distribution problems delayed the release of *The Weight of Water*, which would not have its U.S. premier until July 2001 and did not open in theaters across the country until November 2002. Because of the delays, Bigelow's next film, *K-19: The Widowmaker*, came out before the release of the earlier film. With *K-19: The Widowmaker*, Bigelow turned to a real-life event she found intriguing: a Soviet submarine on a mission to test a nuclear missile. In 1961, during the height of the

Cold War, the submarine K-19 set out for the Arctic. After conducting the missile test, the crew found a leak in the submarine's nuclear reactor. The rapidly heating reactor threatened to set off a nuclear explosion that could have ignited World War III. The Soviets buried the story for almost thirty years— until after the fall of the Berlin Wall.

Bigelow told a reporter that after hearing the story, she was determined to make a movie showing "the heroism, sacrifice, and humanity of these men." During the project, Bigelow and the screenwriter, Christopher Kyle, visited the widow of the K-19's captain in Russia, who greeted them with suspicion. Americans had been considered enemies of the captain's widow's homeland for a good portion of her life. The more the two filmmakers talked with her, however, the more she opened up and shared stories about her husband and their life together. Bigelow said the meeting helped "form a clearer mental picture" of the captain. Before Bigelow and Kyle left, as a symbol of trust, the Russian woman handed Bigelow a portrait of her husband in a large frame. At the door she hugged Bigelow and, sobbing, told her that she must tell her husband's story to the world.

"From that moment on," Bigelow related, "all bets were off. Nothing could stop us. Not even the vagaries of Hollywood." One "vagary" of Hollywood, however, threatened to stop the project before it began. As Bigelow made the rounds trying to finance the film, one studio boss after another asked where the American heroes were in the story. There were none—every character was Russian. Because of this, Hollywood produced no takers. Bigelow then made the film with backing from the National Geographic Society. It was the first major motion picture sponsored by the scientific organization.

A Closed Society

Like *The Loveless* and *Point Break, K-19: The Widowmaker* explores a closed society of men. Bigelow again showed her talent for action and suspense in the screen version of the tale. The thriller captures the feeling of being trapped within the tight quarters of the submarine. The audience senses the growing dread as the men realize the danger posed by the leaking radiation. The movie also details the tensions between the former captain of the submarine, played by Liam Neeson, and the officer sent to replace him—a role filled by Harrison Ford. Both men remain aboard the boat while the struggle between them increases the crew's already high anxiety.

As in Bigelow's other films, the audience knows little of the characters other than their response to the situation aboard the submarine. Only one woman, the young fiancée of the crew's newest member, makes a brief appearance before the boat leaves port. She is seen again in a photograph the boatman clings to, as he lies dying. Almost all the rest of the film is shot inside the submarine. When the men emerge onto the Arctic ice to celebrate the success of the missile test, it's as if a pressure valve has opened.

The tension among the men eases but only briefly. Soon the crew discovers that the cooling system in the reactor has failed. Without the necessary repairs, a nuclear explosion will kill everyone aboard and possibly trigger a nuclear war. The only way to repair the damage is for crewmen to weld pipes inside the reactor. The volunteers face the horror of intentionally exposing themselves to

The cast of *K-19: The Widowmaker*, with Bigelow
(second from right).

deadly levels of radiation. Bigelow shows the first
two crewmen vomiting and in severe pain as they
leave the reactor, their faces swollen with burns.
The next two heroes enter the compartment
knowing that they, too, will be sickened and burned.

In the end the repairs are successful, saving the
world from nuclear disaster. The crew is then taken
aboard another Russian submarine and brought
back home. Those who worked on the reactor die
almost immediately from radiation poisoning.
Twenty others die within the year. Because the
accident was kept secret, the heroes of the K-19
received no public honors.

Bigelow contrasts the sea's beauty and light
against the grays of the submarine's dark interior.
The film's epic moment occurs when the submarine
zooms to the surface and bursts through the ice.
The scene is a spectacular example of Bigelow's
ability to use light and action to create the mood.

FILMMAKING BIGELOW STYLE

Kathryn Bigelow often uses the landscape to enhance the action in her films. She will consult a Foam Core model of the scene to study the angles of the surroundings. That helps her determine when and where to zero in on the action and when to focus on a broader view of the landscape.

Bigelow shot the desert scenes in her vampire film *Near Dark* in Coolidge, Arizona, a small town near Phoenix. She works on location as much as possible to capture what she calls "authenticity." She aims to immerse audiences in the action. Real surroundings add to the feeling that the events are actually happening. The location can unexpectedly add elements to the film.

During one scene in *The Hurt Locker*, actor Brian Geraghty hurls a water bottle at a car blocking the path of his Humvee. Bigelow zeroes in on the angry man in the back of the car shaking his fist at the Americans. The cameras then focus on a mangy cat jumping out of the Humvee's path. The incident was not in

the script. The filmmakers had hired neither the angry man nor the cat. Screenwriter Mark Boal, commenting on the scene, noted it as "a great shot." Many of the shots in a Bigelow film are taken with handheld, lightweight cameras. They allow the film crew to get close to the subject and operate in tight quarters. This technique heightens the movie's suspense and allows the audience to see the whole picture from different views. In a shoot-out scene in *Point Break*, Bigelow shows both the shooter and his victim. Beyond that, the director shows a long shot to reveal where the two are standing in relation to each other. In *The Hurt Locker*, the viewer gets a 360-degree view of the street scene where a bomb lies hidden. This technique convinces viewers that threats seem to come from all sides.

Entertainment Weekly called Bigelow's filmmaking style "muscular, efficient, and stripped of false flourishes." In *The Hurt Locker*, the magazine reported, Bigelow "compresses the anxiety and tension of battle into every frame."

Overcoming Challenges

The filming of *K-19* posed enormous challenges. From February through June of 2001 the filmmakers worked at nine locations on three continents. Among them, Moscow, Canada's Lake Winnipeg, and Iceland provided realistic views of the northern landscape and Arctic Sea.

Bigelow and company modified a Russian submarine for the exterior shots of the boat. On the movie set, filming took place in a replica of the sub's interior. The crew had to maneuver cameras and equipment around the sub's cramped quarters. The film also required two destroyers and a second submarine. Cameras mounted on specially built cranes captured views of the open water and the exterior of the submarine. Tugboats ferried the film crew around the site. Inside the boat, only the lighting available on an actual submarine was used.

The K-19: The Widowmaker budget soared to more than $100 million. At the time it was the most expensive independently produced film ever made. The two-hour-eighteen-minute film distributed by Paramount premiered in the United States on July 19, 2002. It opened to big crowds, ranking number four on its opening weekend and showing in 2,828 theaters. However, critics and audiences were lukewarm toward the film. It grossed a little over $35 million in the U.S. market and another $30.5 million in foreign countries. At the end of its fourteen-week run, *K-19: The Widowmaker* had not come near to breaking even.

The critics posed several reasons for the film's failure to attract blockbuster status. *Entertainment Weekly*'s Owen Gleiberman mocked the title as

Ford, Bigelow, and Fiennes.

"ugly" and "incoherent." The critic also found fault with the movie's actors, whom he dismissed as "grim," "stern-faced," and "dour Russian martinet(s)." American audiences did not like the fact that the heroes had been enemies of the United States during the Cold War.

Other critics applauded Bigelow's ability to portray unexpected truths through stories and characters. Andrew O'Hehir, writing in *Salon*, gave Bigelow high praise for her handling of ambiguous situations. In this case, the heroes were Russians who were working for the Communist Party that threatened the annihilation of America. Under Bigelow's direction, the characters are seen as brave men sacrificing their lives for others. O'Hehir credits Bigelow for having the courage to tell a Cold War story with Russians as heroes and with no Americans in sight. Although agreeing with Gleiberman that the film was too grim to be a big hit, O'Hehir said it was nonetheless a "pulse-pounding thriller" that told "a vivid, highly realistic yarn of real-life heroism." After five years without a major motion picture to her credit, *K-19: The Widowmaker* signified a "triumphant comeback" for Bigelow, according to the critic. Ultimately though, the movie's disappointing showing at the box office made it even more difficult for Bigelow to attract a big-time studio to support her next production.

5 BIGELOW'S BIG BREAK

Kathryn Bigelow first saw the work of journalist Mark Boal around 2002. Boal had written an article for *Playboy* that Bigelow made into a series for television. The series, *The Inside*, was a dark, moody look at violent crimes. Created for Fox Television, the show premiered in 2005 and lasted only thirteen episodes.

Boal also wrote about the Iraq War. At the end of 2004, Boal joined other news crews who accompanied U.S. troops on their missions in Iraq. He sent emails to Bigelow from the war zone, and his descriptions of the bomb squad's dangerous job intrigued her.

Bigelow said that Boal "opened up a window" for her on how to make a film based on current events. She decided to walk through that window. The result was *The Hurt Locker*, her award-winning movie about a U.S. bomb squad in Iraq. The movie brought her work to the forefront in ways that none of her other films had done.

Cast members of *The Hurt Locker*, along with Bigelow and writer Mark Boal.

As soon as Boal returned from Iraq, he and Bigelow began work on a script based on his time with the bomb squad. The intense subject matter made the project a good match for Bigelow's skills as a director. The two believed that Americans had no idea what was happening in the war zone. The image of a soldier in a 100-pound suit trying to disarm a bomb, Bigelow told a *Los Angeles Times* reporter, "brings this conflict into sharp focus."

By 2006, the team had produced a script for *The Hurt Locker*. The name of the film comes from slang used by soldiers to describe a place where terrible injuries are inflicted. "If a bomb goes off, you're going to be in the **hurt locker,**" Boal told the *New Yorker*. "It's somewhere you don't want to be."

Bigelow chose not to cast established stars for the film's major roles. Jeremy Renner played the movie's lead, Sergeant First Class William James. Anthony Mackie filled the role of Sergeant J.T. Sanborn, and Brian Geraghty played Specialist Owen Eldridge. "I wanted to keep the faces unfamiliar," she told Peter Keough during an interview with the *Boston Phoenix*. That way, she explained, viewers would not be expecting the big star to survive the war or the lesser-known actors to die. More-established stars Ralph Fiennes and Guy Pearce made only brief appearances in the movie.

Search for Funding

Bigelow sought the $18–$20 million budgeted for the movie through independent sources, as she had for all her films. Her poor box-office track record, the absence of established stars, and the film's subject matter (the Iraq War) limited the number of buyers willing to provide funds. Bigelow, Boal, and Hollywood producer Greg Shapiro agreed to produce the film. Tony Mark served as executive producer. Still, they needed help to meet the budget Bigelow had set for the film.

Nicolas Chartier, owner of Voltage Pictures, liked the script. Voltage usually sold film rights to foreign buyers. Chartier, however, asked to be one of the producers of *The Hurt Locker*. He also convinced several foreign buyers to back the film. His efforts raised enough to pay about a quarter of the film's cost. Grosvenor Park Media, which had financed other independent films, agreed to contribute to the project. Chartier mortgaged his house to raise the final money needed for the film. To make ends meet,

Jeremy Renner, star of *The Hurt Locker*.

the budget was cut to about $13 million. Having independent funding, Bigelow said, allowed her much more freedom in making the film, even with a reduced budget. "We had complete creative control," she told Kingsley Marshall during a 2009 interview with the British movie magazine *Little White Lies*.

With the funding finally in place, filming began in July 2007 and took forty-four days. Bigelow shot in Jordan, not far from the Iraqi border. She insisted on filming on location despite the heat. There was no other way to make the film look authentic, she said. Jordan served as the perfect backdrop. The country also had thousands of refugees from Iraq in nearby camps. Bigelow enlisted them for crowd scenes, as well as Iraqi actors for secondary roles. One, Suhail Aldabbach, portrayed an Arab forced to be a suicide bomber. For almost all the scenes, the crew used four handheld cameras. Bigelow wanted to show the area surrounding the action.

To get the shots she wanted, Bigelow and her crew climbed hills and trekked over desert sands. The temperature soared to 120 degrees Fahrenheit (49 degrees Celsius). The heat posed the biggest challenge to Jeremy Renner, who had to perform in a 100-pound bomb suit. At one point during the filming, Renner fell down a flight of stairs and hurt his ankle. Some crew members suffered from heatstroke.

"War Is a Drug"

The movie opens with a quote from Chris Hedges, a war correspondent and author: "War is a drug." The action begins on a busy street in Baghdad, Iraq, in 2004. Three members of a U.S. bomb squad set out on their mission: to locate and defuse **IEDs (improvised explosive devices)**. Each man has a specific job. The intelligence officer, Sergeant Sanborn, oversees the operation. Specialist Eldridge wields a rifle and provides cover for the rest of the team. Staff Sergeant Thompson (Guy Pearce) and later Sergeant James defuse the bombs.

In this first scene, the camera speeds along a dirt roadway in jerky, blurry motion. In the background a man shouts in Arabic as people run to avoid a Humvee filled with armed men. The scene is overrun by chaos. The camera zooms in to reveal the looks of concentration on the squad members' faces. Sanborn, Eldridge, and Thompson send out a remote-controlled device to patrol the area for IEDs. A bomb is spotted—a robot on a motorized wagon sets out to detonate it. A wheel falls off the wagon, and it sits in the middle of the street. Sanborn and Eldridge help Thompson get into his bomb suit. He walks toward the bomb then crouches to work on it. With each image and each step, the tension builds until it is almost unbearable.

Too late the squad sees a man with a cell phone among the city's onlookers—he presses a button. Thompson runs but not far enough. His bulky suit is no match for the force of the explosion. In slow motion his body hits the ground. The camera zooms in on the dead soldier's face. Blood trickles slowly down the side of his helmet visor. The message, critic Jeannette Catsoulis notes in the film journal *Reverse Shot*, is that "hi-tech clothing can protect your flesh, but war kills most efficiently from the inside."

A new staff sergeant, James, takes Thompson's place on the squad. On his first mission, he reveals himself as a risk-taker who ignores the rules. He is addicted to the adrenaline rush brought on by his work. Meanwhile, Eldridge and Sanborn have begun the countdown for the remaining thirty-eight

Bigelow directing in the sand on the set of *The Hurt Locker*, 2008.

days on their tour. They want to get out of Iraq alive. The movie follows the team through seven episodes. Each one has a new horror. In one scene, James unearths one bomb—only to follow the wires to reveal six more bombs circling him in the sand. In other scenes, the squad has to deal with bombs tied to a terrified man and buried inside the body of a dead child. Through it all, the film focuses on the characters. Unlike some war movies, *The Hurt Locker* is not political. It takes no side, for or against, the Iraq War. The movie is more about the men and war's effects on them than about the war itself. It is based on Boal's observations during his time with a bomb squad in Iraq. The events and the characters, however, are fictitious.

Renner is much more complex than the swaggering hero he first appears to be. Near the end of the movie, after the men have returned home, Renner realizes he does not fit into his old life with his wife and son. A trip to the grocery store to buy cereal overwhelms him. He cannot decide which box to get. In the final scene, Renner returns to Iraq to the job he does best. The clock then starts ticking down the next 365 days of his tour.

The Hurt Locker captures an overwhelming sense of danger and anxiety. Bigelow uses slow motion to stop the action and build tension. Shaky camera work and extreme close-ups increase the intensity and make the scenes seem real. A fly crawls across a giant eyeball. A seemingly huge shell casing slowly falls to the ground.

Without the clout of one of Hollywood's big studios to get her movie shown in theaters across the country, Bigelow followed a different route. She took *The Hurt Locker* to film festivals worldwide to generate interest. On September 4, 2008,

The Hurt Locker premiered at the Venice International Film Festival in Italy. At the end of the screening, the audience rose and clapped for ten minutes. The film came away with four awards, including Venice's prestigious SIGNIS Award. A jury of young cinema buffs in attendance named *The Hurt Locker* its choice as best film in the competition.

The Hurt Locker had its North American premiere at Toronto's international film festival only four days after its triumph in Venice. A host of other honors followed at festivals from Boston to Seattle, and from Australia to Finland to Romania. The screenings brought an avalanche of praise from critics. *Time* magazine called it "a near-perfect movie about men in war." *Miami Herald* movie critic Rene Rodriguez described the film as "a masterpiece," "a great action movie," and Bigelow's "greatest triumph." Critic Roger Ebert rated it second on a list of the top ten films of the decade. *Hurt Locker*, Ebert wrote, is "a triumph of theme and execution, and very nearly flawless." As Bigelow had hoped, the acclaim grabbed the attention of movie executives. After the Toronto festival, Summit Entertainment paid $1.5 million to distribute the film in the United States.

The Hurt Locker's Hollywood premiere was held June 5, 2009. Its distribution was limited to 535 movie houses in part because war movies typically do not attract the same number of moviegoers as other genres. Also, American audiences thought the movie was too intense.

Honors and Accolades

The financial disappointments didn't harm the film's reputation. In December 2009, the New York Film

Bigelow showing off her DGA award.

Critics named Bigelow best director, and *The Hurt Locker* best film of the year. On January 24, 2010, the Producers Guild of America selected *The Hurt Locker* as best theatrical motion picture. Six days later, Bigelow became the first woman ever to receive the Directors Guild of America's top award.

The honor stirred talk that Bigelow would also win the Oscar. **The Academy of Motion Picture Arts and Sciences** had never in its 82-year-history presented the statue to a woman director. On February 2, the Academy announced its nominees—*The Hurt Locker* earned nine. The film tied with *Avatar*, James Cameron's hugely popular 3-D science fiction epic. Both movies, facing stiff competition, made the cut for best film. For the first time since 1943, the Academy nominated ten

Bigelow, Boal, and *The Hurt Locker* cast at the Oscars.

movies for best picture. Cameron and Bigelow were nominated for best director. Reporters made much of the fact that the two had been married and divorced. Stories about the "battle of the exes" appeared in entertainment journals.

The audience waited for the announcement of best director. Cameras zeroed in on Bigelow and Cameron, who was seated behind her. When Barbra Streisand read Bigelow's name, Cameron patted his ex-wife on the back. The audience exploded in cheers as the first woman to win the award made her way to the stage. Breathless, Bigelow thanked the members of the Academy for "the moment of a lifetime." Crediting Boal for his "courageous screenplay," she said that he had "risked his life for the words on the page." She ended her short speech by dedicating the award "to the women and men in the military who risk their lives on a daily basis in Iraq and Afghanistan and around the world." She added: "May they come home safe."

Members of *The Hurt Locker* team made five more trips to the stage to collect awards. The Oscar for best screenplay went to Boal. Chris Innis and Bob Murawski received the best editing prize, and Paul Ottosson won for best sound editing and shared a prize for best sound mixing with Ray Beckett. The second big win for Bigelow came when actor Tom Hanks announced *The Hurt Locker* as the year's best picture. The director walked from backstage clutching one golden statue to accept the second. Boal and producer Greg Shapiro joined her on stage to collect their own Oscars. Jeremy Renner, Anthony Mackie, and Brian Geraghty, the three actors who portrayed the members of the bomb squad, stood behind them, cheering and raising their fists in triumph.

6 CONTROVERSY AND ACCLAIM

The Academy Awards thrust Kathryn Bigelow into the limelight and introduced her films to many more viewers. However, the fanfare did little to boost the movie's box-office earnings. Ultimately, the film's take from U.S. theaters amounted only to about $17 million. *The Hurt Locker* earned almost $50 million worldwide and another $49 million in video sales. In contrast, *Avatar* earned about $2.6 billion in U.S. and global sales by March 2010.

Winning the Oscar did make it easier for Bigelow to find investors in her next film. Shortly after the awards, she and Mark Boal won the backing of Paramount Pictures, one of Hollywood's larger studios, for another joint project. The new action film would focus on the drug trade in South America. The project stalled after disagreements over casting, budget, and other issues, however.

Boal began working on a script focused on America's failed attempts to capture Al Qaeda leader Osama bin Laden in 2001, who headed the terrorist

Zero Dark Thirty film crew on location in India.

group behind the September 11, 2001, attacks on the United States. Bigelow wanted to be free of the strings attached to a studio-sponsored film. She secured the backing of Megan Ellison, whose father, Larry Ellison, is the billionaire cofounder of Oracle, a global software company. The film's entire budget of $45 million came from her funds.

Change of Direction

Boal had made quite a bit of progress on the script when an unexpected event changed everything. On May 1, 2011, President Barack Obama announced that U.S. forces had just killed bin Laden at his hideout in Pakistan. Bigelow and Boal decided to rewrite the script—this version centered on America's successful mission to locate bin Laden. The new version was completed in record time. Filming began less than a year after the actual mission took place. "There was a kind of urgency in the timeliness of [the film]," Bigelow said during a 2012 press conference on the movie.

Bigelow and Boal returned to Jordan for some of the filming. Other scenes were shot in India and London. It took from March to early June to film the project.

The movie's name, **Zero Dark Thirty**, is military slang for 12:30 a.m., the time of the raid. Even before the movie was titled, it came under fire. Sony Pictures had signed on as the film's distributor. The film company's CEO, Michael Lynton, had supported Obama during his 2008 presidential race. That fueled rumors that the filmmakers aimed to release the movie in time to influence the 2012 election. As it turned out, the film did not open until well after the election.

Members of Congress questioned whether Boal and Bigelow had had improper access to government secrets, charging that Boal had been given classified information. Critics including U.S. Senator John McCain also accused the filmmakers of promoting the use of torture and falsely implying that torture led to bin Laden's capture. They claimed that such abuses did not play a role in the CIA's hunt for bin Laden.

The Senate Intelligence Committee conducted an investigation into the matters in January 2013. Six weeks later the committee dropped the probe without comment.

Based on Events

Like *The Hurt Locker, Zero Dark Thirty* focuses on characters. Most are a blend of fiction and fact derived from real people who participated in the hunt. Boal and Bigelow insist that the script and the movie are based on "firsthand accounts of actual events." The fact that several women led the effort to track down bin Laden surprised Boal. Maya, the lead character, Boal said, was based on "a real person, but she also represents the work of a lot of other women." He said many of the agents still work for the CIA.

As in other films, Bigelow reveals her characters' nature through their on-screen actions. She chooses not to spend time exploring a character's past because it "takes time away" from the main story. "It pierces the momentum," she explains.

Zero Dark Thirty opens with a black screen. Viewers hear frantic cell phone messages of rescue workers and people trapped after terrorists crashed planes into the World Trade Center's Twin Towers on September 11, 2001. The eerie reality of the heartbreaking calls sets the tone for the film.

In the next scenes CIA agents torture a suspect named Ammar, played by Reda Kateb. He endures humiliation and pain at the hands of his captor, Dan, played by Jason Clarke. The agents nearly drown Ammar, prevent him from sleeping, and withhold food. They want Ammar to reveal information about bin Laden, but he refuses. CIA agent Maya, played by Jessica Chastain, has just arrived at the secret base and witnesses the abuse. She has spent her entire career trying to track down bin Laden. When she is left in charge, she does not back away from the task at hand. In the midst of the ten-year search for bin Laden, Obama replaces George W. Bush as U.S. president. The change in command signals a shift away from torture to more subtle means of gathering information.

FILMING A SPECTACULAR SHOW

From marketplaces teeming with people to specially built helicopters landing in the dead of night, *Zero Dark Thirty* posed enormous challenges for the filmmakers. The movie's huge crowd scenes took place in India, near the border with Pakistan. To film the shots required a bit of trickery. Bigelow did not want passersby to look at the camera while she was filming the crowd, so she set up a decoy film crew at another location on the street. An actor not in the real scene put on a show for the camera. While people were looking at the fake scene, another camera crew filmed the real action. When the crowd began to figure out what was taking place, Bigelow had the decoy crew begin filming the real scenes.

It took four weeks to film the raid on bin Laden's hideout. The scene required enormous preparation and equipment. To make the raid look as real as possible, Bigelow filmed through night-vision goggles, which were difficult to get through customs into Jordan. The camera crew then had to figure out how

to adjust with almost no lighting filtered through the goggles' green haze.

Workers built a full-size three-story building to duplicate bin Laden's compound. It had to be sturdy enough to withstand the wind from nearby helicopters. Fitting everyone into the confines of the rooms created other problems. There were 150 crew members, twenty-two in the cast. Actors and crew with cameras and other equipment had to race through doors, across floors, and up two flights of stairs. Workers also built two helicopters for the scene. The stealth helicopters used in the real raid are a state secret, so they had to guess what the aircraft might have looked like. When Bigelow shouted the final "Cut!" it took two editors to review the two million feet of film shot for the movie.

While being questioned, a suspect mentions the name of a man to Maya. After uncovering more information, she suspects that the man is linked to bin Laden. Further investigation leads to the villa where Maya believes the terrorist leader is hiding. Once she convinces her bosses—not an easy task— a team of Navy SEALs raids the compound.

The nighttime raid is an amazing feat—both the real operation and Bigelow's film rendition of it. The SEALs arrive in helicopters in total darkness. They storm the compound, search the rooms, shoot or disarm those who resist, and finally shoot and kill bin Laden. Seen through the SEALs' night-vision goggles, the scenes are surreal and intense.

By November 18, 2012, the filmmakers had finished production work on the movie. It opened in a few theaters on December 19. On January 10, 2013, the Academy of Motion Picture Arts and Sciences announced that *Zero Black Thirty* was a nominee for that year's best picture award. Chastain was nominated for best actress, and Boal collected a nomination for best screenplay. The movie also earned two more nominations: sound editing and film editing.

A "Must-See" Movie

The next day Sony released *Zero Dark Thirty* to 2,937 theaters nationwide. The controversy surrounding the film coupled with the Oscar nominations made it a "must-see" movie. Audiences flocked to view it. It topped the charts on its first weekend of showing nationally, earning more than $24 million in ticket sales. During its 14.7-week run, *Zero Dark Thirty* grossed $95.7 million, with another $37.1 million coming from foreign sales.

Bigelow at the BAFTA award ceremony.

Critics raved and film groups showered the film with awards. Bigelow was nominated as best director by dozens of film organizations worldwide, including the Golden Globes, the Directors Guild of America, and the British Academy of Film and Television Awards (BAFTA).

Bigelow won BAFTA's Britannia Award for excellence in directing, and picked up best director honors from the National Board of Review. The Writers Guild of America chose Boal for its best original screenplay award. However, the film won only one Oscar, none by Bigelow.

Bigelow has not yet announced what her next project will be. However, she hinted that it will be another entry into current events. "Once you've opened the window on topical material," she told *Time* reporter Jessica Winter, "it's very hard to close it."

FILMOGRAPHY

The following is a list of the theatrical releases Kathryn Bigelow has directed, written, produced, or acted in as of the end of 2013. The films are listed in alphabetical order by year. For a more complete listing, including her television work, please visit the Internet Movie Database website, www.IMDb.com

The Set-Up (short) (1978 / director)

The Loveless (1981/ director / writer)

Born in Flames (1983 / actor)

Near Dark (1987 / director / writer)

Blue Steel (1989 / director / writer)

Point Break (1991 / director)

Strange Days (1995 / director)

Undertow (TV movie) (1995 / director / co-writer)

The Weight of Water (2000 / director)

K-19: The Widowmaker (2002 / director / producer)

The Hurt Locker (2008 / director / producer)

Zero Dark Thirty (2012 / director / producer)

GLOSSARY

abstract expressionism—An art form that uses abstract images (those that do not look like real objects or people) to evoke emotional feelings.

Academy of Motion Picture Arts and Sciences—Awards Oscars each year to top performers in a number of movie categories.

box office—The money collected from movie ticket sales.

cinematography—Photography used in making a movie.

commodities trader—A person who buys and sells certain goods, such as gold.

conceptual art—A form of art that focuses on the ideas behind a piece of art rather than on the artwork itself.

contemporary art—Works of art that are produced in present times.

director—The person who oversees and directs the making of a movie.

form (in art)—A medium of expression in fine art, such as dance or sculpture.

genre—A category or class of art or film that share certain traits or styles.

GLOSSARY

gross—The total amount of money a movie earns.

haiku—A short Japanese poem using imagery.

hurt locker—A place associated with pain and injury.

improvised explosive devices (IEDs)—A homemade bomb constructed to incapacitate personnel or vehicles.

lead—The starring role in a movie or play.

National Endowment for the Arts—A federal agency that funds and supports art and creativity.

New Wave—Popularized especially in the 1970s and 1980s, this style of music possesses strong, exaggerated beats, unconventional melodies, quirky lyrics, and uses many electronic instruments.

Oscar—The gold statue awarded each year by the Academy of Motion Picture Arts and Sciences for top achievers in movies.

performance art—A presentation or show that accompanies visual art, such as a painting or sculpture.

producer—The person in charge of providing, or arranging for, the money to make a movie.

short—A short film; one not as long as a traditional movie.

zero dark thirty—A military term referring to 12:30 a.m.

BIBLIOGRAPHY

Diamond, Jamie. "Kathryn Bigelow Pushes the Potentiality Envelope," *New York Times*, October 22, 1995.

Duray, Dan. "Point Break: As Oscar Calls, a Look at Kathryn Bigelow's Decade in the NYC Art World." *Galleristny.com*

Hill, Logan. "Secrets of 'Zero Dark Thirty.'" *Rolling Stone.com*

Jermyn, Deborah, and Sean Redmond, eds. *The Cinema of Kathryn Bigelow: Hollywood Transgressor.* London, England: Wallflower Press, 2003.

Keough, Peter, ed. *Kathryn Bigelow: Interviews.* Jackson, MS: University Press of Mississippi, 2013.

"Letter from Director Kathryn Bigelow." *National Geographic.* www.nationalgeographic.com/k19/director.html.

Steele, Jeff. "Nicolas Chartier and the Hidden Hands Who Financed 'The Hurt Locker.'" *Film Closings*, March 6, 2010. filmclosings.com/2010/03/hidden-hands-on-the-hurt-locker.

Welsh, James Michael, and Donald M. Whaley. *The Oliver Stone Encyclopedia.* Lanham, MD: Scarecrow Press Inc., 2013.

SOURCE NOTES

Chapter 1

Pg. 4: Winter, Jessica, "Cover Story: Kathryn Bigelow's Art of Darkness," *Time*, January 24, 2013.

Pg. 11: *Artforum*, 1995, cited in Dan Duray, "Point Break: As Oscar Calls, a Look at Kathryn Bigelow's Decade in the NYC Art World," *Galleristny.com*, February 5, 2013.

Chapter 2

Pg. 18: Horn, John, "Five Acclaimed Directors Speak Directly," *Los Angeles Times*, January 21, 2010.

Pg. 21: Miller, John M., "Near Dark," Turner Classic Movies, www.tcm.com/this-month/article.html?isPreview=&id=382629|491987&name=Near-Dark

Pg. 21: *Empire* [no author], "Near Dark: Impressive genre-twisting debut from Bigelow," *Empireonline.com*.

Pgs. 24–25: Taylor, Clarke, "Black-Leather Director in a Business World: Cult Favorite Kathryn Bigelow Brings Her 'Dark' Style to an Action Film," *Los Angeles Times*, October 9, 1988.

Pg. 27: Welsh, James Michael, and Donald M. Whaley, *The Oliver Stone Encyclopedia* (Lanham, MD: Scarecrow Press Inc., 2013), pp. 20–21.

Pg. 27: Ebert, Roger, "Blue Steel," March 16, 1990, www.rogerebert.com/reviews/blue-steel-1990.

Pg. 27: Turan, Kenneth, "Blue Steel," *Los Angeles Times*, cited in Kathryn Bigelow: Interviews, p. 43.

Pg. 27: Floyd, Nigel, "Blue Steel," *TimeOut*, www.timeout.com/london/film/blue-steel.

Chapter 3

Pg. 31: Jermyn, Deborah, and Sean Redmond, eds. *The Cinema of Kathryn Bigelow: Hollywood Transgressor*, p. 23.

Pg. 33: Keough, *Kathryn Bigelow: Interviews*, p. 37.

Chapter 4

Pg. 41: Jermyn and Redmond, eds. *The Cinema of Kathryn Bigelow: Hollywood Transgressor*, p.12.

Pg. 41: Bigelow, Kathryn, "Letter from Director Kathryn Bigelow," *K-19: The Widowmaker*, *National Geographic*, 1996.

Pg. 41: Bigelow, "Letter from Director Kathryn Bigelow."

Pg. 45: *The Hurt Locker*, directed by Kathryn Bigelow (2008; Santa Monica, CA: Summit Entertainment, 2010), DVD.

Pg. 45: Gleiberman, Owen, " *K-19: The Widowmaker* (2002)," *Entertainment Weekly*, July 17, 2002, www.ew.com/ew/article/0,,321572,00.html.

Chapter 5

Pg. 48: Winter, "Cover Story: Kathryn Bigelow's Art of Darkness."

Pg. 50: Whipp, Glenn, "Kathryn Bigelow and the making of 'The Hurt Locker,'" *Los Angeles Times*, December 23, 2009.

Pg. 50: *New Yorker*, [no author], "Inside the Hurt Locker," *The New Yorker*, July 10, 2009, www.newyorker.com/online/blogs/newsdesk/2009/07/inside-the-hurt-locker.html.

Pg. 51: Keough, Peter, "An Interview with Kathryn Bigelow," *Boston Phoenix*, July 4, 2009, cited in *Kathryn Bigelow: Interviews*, p. 179.

Pg. 52: Marshall, Kingsley, "*The Hurt Locker* Interview: Kathryn Bigelow and Mark Boal," *Little White Lies*, September 1, 2009, p. 202.

Pg. 53: *The Hurt Locker*, directed by Kathryn Bigelow, 2008 (Santa Monica, CA: Summit Entertainment, 2010), DVD.

Pg. 54: Catsoulis, Jeannette, "War Is Swell," *Reverse Shot*, Issue 25, 2009, www.reverseshot.com/article/hurt_locker.

Pg. 56: Corliss, Richard, "*The Hurt Locker*: A Near-Perfect War Film," *Time*, September 4, 2008.

Pg. 56: Rodriguez, Rene, "Review: 'The Hurt Locker,'" *Miami Herald*, July 23, 2009, miamiherald. typepad.com/reeling/2009/07/review-the-hurt-locker.html.

Pg. 56: Ebert, Roger, "The Best Films of the Decade," *Roger Ebert's Journal,* December 30, 2009, www. rogerebert.com/rogers-journal/the-best-films-of-the-decade.

Pg. 59: "Kathryn Bigelow's 2010 Oscar Acceptance Speech," March 7, 2010, Academy of Motion Picture Arts and Sciences, www.oscars.org/ awards/academyawards/legacy/ceremony/82nd. html.

Chapter 6

Pg. 63: Keough, Peter, and Brett Michel, "Press Conference for *Zero Dark Thirty*," pp. 225–226.

Pg. 63: Keough and Michel, "Press Conference for *Zero Dark Thirty*."

Pg. 63: *Zero Dark Thirty*, directed by Kathryn Bigelow, 2012 (Culver City, CA: Sony Pictures Home Entertainment, 2013), DVD.

Pgs. 64–65: Hill, Logan, "Secrets of 'Zero Dark Thirty,'" *Rolling Stone*, January 11, 2013.

Pg. 67: Winter, "Cover Story: Kathryn Bigelow: The Art of Darkness."

FURTHER INFORMATION

Books

Frost, Shelley. *Kids Guide to Movie Making: How Kids Can Produce and Direct Their Own Movies That Audiences Will Love*. San Carlos, CA: Make-A-Movie Studios, 2011.

Grabham, Tim, Suridh Hassan, Dave Reeve, and Clare Richards. *Movie Maker: The Ultimate Guide to Making Films*. Somerville, MA: Candlewick Press, 2010.

Kinney, Jeff. *The Wimpy Kid Movie Diary*. New York: Abrams Books, 2010.

Klise, Kate. *Hollywood, Dead Ahead (43 Old Cemetery Road)*. New York: Houghton Mifflin Harcourt, 2013.

Krossing, Karen. *Cut the Lights*. Custer, WA: Orca Book Publishers, 2013.

Lanier, Troy, and Clay Nichols. *Filmmaking for Teens: Pulling Off Your Shorts*. Studio City, CA: Wiese, Michael Productions, 2010.

O'Neill, Joseph. *Movie Director* (21st Century Skills Library: Cool Careers). North Mankato, MN: Cherry Lake Publishing, 2013.

Piercy, Helen. *Animation Studio*. Somerville, MA: Candlewick Press, 2013.

Telgemeier, Raina. *Drama*. New York: Scholastic, Graphix, 2012.

Williams, Dar. *Lights, Camera, Amalee*. Grand Haven, MI: Brilliance Audio, 2011.

On the Web
www.boxoffice.com
www.boxofficemojo.com
These websites contain financial data such as box-office grosses and other information on movies including showtime and release schedules.

www.imdb.com
The Internet Movie Database contains a plethora of information on movie trends, directors, celebrity news, and film trailers.

www.newyorker.com
Search *The New Yorker* for many articles on Kathryn Bigelow and her films.

www.oscars.org
Explore the science of movies, cinematography in the Digital Age, and archived films. Learn about the history and organization of the Academy Awards through the Academy Museum of Motion Pictures on this website.

www.time.com
Explore *Time* magazine's website and uncover several great articles on Kathryn Bigelow and her movies.

INDEX

Page numbers in **boldface** are illustrations.

ABOUT THE AUTHOR

Susan Dudley Gold is a writer, historian, and movie buff. She has written several books that feature women and their roles in current events, including *Roberts v. U.S. Jaycees: Women's Rights*. She is the author of two books in Cavendish Square's Great Filmmakers series—*Kathyrn Bigelow* and *Sofia Coppola*—and five books for the publisher's First Amendment Cases series.

In the 1980s, Gold produced, directed, and wrote a thirty-minute video, "The 10th Year: Maine's Fishing Industry, 1976–1985," which was screened at the statewide Maine Fishermen's Forum.

Gold worked as a newspaper reporter and magazine editor before becoming a graphic designer and children's book author. She has written more than fifty books for middle- and high-school students on a wide range of topics. She has received numerous honors for her writing and design work, including a Carter G. Woodson Honor Book award for *United States v. Amistad: Slave Ship Mutiny* (Supreme Court Milestones).

Gold and her husband own a web design and publishing business in Maine. They have one son and two grandchildren.